P9-DYE-775

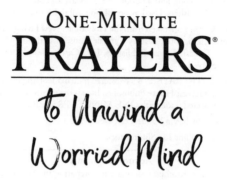

ONE-MINUTE
PRAYERS®
to Unwind a Worried Mind

Hope Lyda

HARVEST HOUSE PUBLISHERS
EUGENE, OREGON

Cover Design by Kevin VanderLeak Design Inc.

Cover photo © Elina Li / Shutterstock

Acknowledgments

Thank you to Kimberly Shumate for preparing the Scripture foundation. Your presence and talent are gifts to me. And thank you to Harvest House who believes in creating books like this. A shout out to my family and friends who understand the woes and the humor of the anxious heart. Last of all…thank you, Quiet Jesus. You love and center me when the thoughts begin to tangle.   —Hope

One-Minute Prayers® to Unwind a Worried Mind

Contents

We do not know what to do, but our eyes are on you.

2 CHRONICLES 20:12

Why, my soul, are you downcast?
Why so disturbed within me? Put your hope in God.

Psalm 43:5

Unwind Your Worried Mind

How do our thoughts get so tangled? Some days our initially linear ideas and goals are sabotaged by worries and twisted by what-ifs. Forget the rabbit trail tangents of old; our contemporary woes now appear and tumble much faster than hops and leaps. They keep up with our frenetic pace. But our skill to *be still* lags. The worries become intertwined and nearly indistinguishable from one another.

God is waiting for us to pause in and pray through the worry. The spiritual practice of bringing our knotted thoughts to him is transforming. At first it feels like throwing an impossibly huge ball of yarn to our creator. (A ball of yarn after 20 cats have played with it and then tried to roll it back up with their claws activated, that is.) God is up for the challenge. He'll unwind our worried minds and create a strong thread of peace-giving communication with him no matter what our circumstances present.

Start a new habit of praying through those burdens you want to release, like fear and anxiety, as well as for the blessings you long to have, such as provision and hope. May this be a journey of releasing and receiving that leads you to trust in God's care.

You See Them Coming

You know when I sit and when I rise;
you perceive my thoughts from afar.

PSALM 139:2

What do my worries look like, sound like, feel like to you, God? You see everything. By the time I hesitantly lift a worry to you, you've already seen it, weighed it, shed some light on it. The muddled mass of troubles doesn't faze you. Your hands remain outstretched to receive because you want me to have peace.

Today I begin a practice that will become as ordinary as getting out of bed and selecting the strongest brew setting on the coffeemaker: I'll give you this day's worries. I'll entrust to you these humble pieces of me you've seen coming and that you're already tending to in your mercy.

PROVISION

May you lead me to your
care and abundance, Lord.

All I Need

*Take nothing for the journey except a staff—no
bread, no bag, no money in your belts.*

MARK 6:8

Provider. That's who you are, God, even when I don't initially see all that comes from your hand. You sent the disciples to share your word with nothing in their possession except a staff. The journey wouldn't be easy, but they would move forward unencumbered, and all they needed would be provided. Lord, let this ease my anxious thoughts. When I stress about not having enough, give me eyes to see all you've given along the way: friends, family, belongings, a home, food, opportunities, work, connections, physical abilities, times of ministry. Everything comes from you.

Whatever I list right now as a thing I "desperately want but don't yet have" is also one less burden while I walk in faith and do the work you call me to.

Provision of Redemption

*I know that through your prayers and God's provision
of the Spirit of Jesus Christ
what has happened to me will turn
out for my deliverance.*

PHILIPPIANS 1:19

I am never left to perish in my circumstances, because of your grace, Lord. You don't exile me to the place where my weaknesses can never be transformed in your mercy and power. You have provided your children with the Spirit of Christ to guide and deliver us no matter what we face or what we try to create in our meager power.

When struggles come because the resources are few and the wants are many, you redeem my heart's hunger. When I mistakenly count my possessions instead of counting my blessings, you redeem my poor spirit. And when I suffer from the belief that I'm not worthy of deliverance, you breathe your Spirit into my brokenness, and redemption is my story.

Soul Security

*Better a little with the fear of the LORD
than great wealth with turmoil.*

PROVERBS 15:16

Lord, give me wisdom to trust only you for my peace and security. My list of just-in-case hopes is filled with tangibles and provisions shaped by the unpredictable world. Life changes, and so does the dependability of jobs, income, savings, and all factors tied to limited human power.

You, Lord, are not limited. You are the source of my hope and my help. You are my sole and soul security. The reverence I have for you leads me to appreciate all that comes from you. I watch for the gifts you bring into my life through others and along the path you lead me. When the winds of change do blow, I'm not worried about having or losing plenty. Even with little, I can stand securely on your foundation of faith, truth, grace, and love.

Speaking from Plenty

*I am not saying this because I am in need,
for I have learned to be
content whatever the circumstances.*

PHILIPPIANS 4:11

God, the words and prayers looping through my mind are so often about discontentment and what's missing. Often, I want something other than what I have.

Yet I know you and love you as the well of resource and replenishment for every need in my spirit and life. Let this be the truth I walk in, talk from, and live out. Give me a strong sense of your expansive grace and abundance. I want to use language reflecting the wealth of hope I have in you. I trust you for each minute and detail. Shift the words of my heart toward assurance and peace so the words of my mouth speak from your plenty. May I live from this generously.

FORGIVENESS

May I surrender to your grace
and live boldly from it.

Let It Be Known

*All the prophets testify about him
that everyone who believes in him
receives forgiveness of sins through his name.*

ACTS 10:43

Jesus, your name transforms and redeems. When I hear it mentioned or speak it aloud, my heart softens and my tension eases. Your presence turns concerns to peace. When more troubles come, I can call on your name and stand on the foundation of who you are.

You alone forgive me, heal my spirit, and renew my mind. How great are your gifts. And these gifts are not for me alone but for all who believe in you. Lord, I will let it be known to friends and strangers that I walk through this life clothed in mercy. May I testify to your power by humbly revealing my dependence on you for everything.

Moved

In him we live and move and have our being.
ACTS 17:28

made it from birth until now. I made it from last month to this month. I made it from the starting line of a trial to the finish line of relief. But, of course, I didn't really "do" any of that, because you are the force that guides me and the presence where I abide.

In hindsight, I clearly see those times when my preoccupation with worries has hindered the gift of being moved by you through an experience. Forgive me for times when I resist being redirected from sins, self-pity, or anger toward renewed life. I truly want to reside in your redemption. Today I place my trust in you and surrender to what will be and who I'm becoming. Move me, Lord. I am yours.

Returning

I have swept away your offenses like a cloud,
your sins like the morning mist.
Return to me, for I have redeemed you.

ISAIAH 44:22

This has been a "two steps forward and three steps back" kind of life season, Lord. I want to be closer to you. In my weariness, my default thoughts are a running list of regrets. I'm ready to put down my plans and stand before you to be washed clean. You sweep away my past offenses and wipe away both my tears and my transgressions. It's amazing how heavy those had become. I feel the forgiveness in my spirit and in every cell. I am feather light and shiny new. You extend your arms, and I bow in gratitude. But I see you are motioning for me to come into your embrace. This is the homecoming we have both longed for.

Patient Grace

*You, Lord, are a compassionate and gracious God,
slow to anger,
abounding in love and faithfulness.*

PSALM 86:15

Have you noticed my state of disarray lately, Lord? Here I am holding up the messy pieces of my troubled mind and the wreckage of plans gone wrong. Again. I need you to fix it. And by "it," I mean me and my desire to push the limits and refuse the initial help you offer.

I am wiser than this; I know it. Others even seek me out for wisdom and spiritual nourishment. But I spend much of my time as the child who hasn't quite learned the faith lessons you present patiently for me to count as wisdom. You are not angry. Instead you take my strange offering of failures with gentle grace. With patience you show me how even the brokenness is part of my purposed life because it brings me back to you and your faithfulness.

REGRET

May I release my regrets to
receive your hope.

Free Spirit

*The Lord is the Spirit, and where the
Spirit of the Lord is, there is freedom.*

2 CORINTHIANS 3:17

Lord, I long for my prayer dialogues and my interactions with others to be centered on you as Spirit
and as Presence. When my life is compartmentalized,
worries take over. Without realizing it, I keep regrets
distant from the influence of faith. I believe in the freedom and grace found in you, yet I live with parts of
me closed off. Sometimes it hurts too much to expose
them. Other times I'm so immersed in today's concerns that dragging a past regret to your attention seems
a waste of time.

But it isn't. Ever. I will release what I have kept
hidden. Let the goodness you're breathing into my life
expand into *all* parts of me. I want to be a free spirit in
you, Spirit.

Confessions of an Inconsistent Confessor

If we confess our sins,
he is faithful and just and will forgive us our
sins and purify us from all unrighteousness.

1 John 1:9

I confess I don't confess my sins very much, God. (But you already know this.) It's the part of the forgiveness equation I find easy to sidestep when my mind is preoccupied with family and life matters. But when I pause and think about my transgressions or notice I'm turning the same regrets over and over in my heart, my spirit wants to share about these. I feel compelled to come to you with these wounds or wounds-in-the-making.

Bringing each of these to you in prayer becomes a privilege and a freedom, not a rigid step in a cold process. You gather my confessions in your hands of grace and forgive me. Regret has no foothold when I surrender to your righteousness. Thank you, Lord.

A Perfect Imperfect

We all stumble in many ways.

JAMES 3:2

My stumbles have been significant. I've tripped over my tongue and stopped and dropped over doubts. I've run into regrets and fallen over faults. I consider myself a talented tumbler after many years of this ongoing act. But this "talent" does not define me. I am graceful in and through your grace. These past blunders aren't preserved for eternity, because they've been pulled from the replay reel. I occasionally return to them when my mind insists on reliving regret.

But you, Lord, don't want me dwelling in this fallen state. You ask me to follow you without worrying whether I'll stumble on my way to the foot of the cross. Whichever imperfect way I get to your presence becomes perfect the minute I arrive.

The Way Out

Turn from evil and do good; seek peace and pursue it.

Psalm 34:14

'm eager to live from a place of gladness. For too long I have wandered with a shadow over me. I wasn't living true to your Word and true to the hope you planted in me, Lord. I was tempted to believe the voice that whispered I would always be someone who fumbled along in the dark without a purpose or a chance to escape into light.

Now I turn my face to you. Joy brightens my outlook and illuminates the way out of my past and my worries. The steps forward are suddenly visible. You tell me I'm worthy to pursue your light and to believe in this peace because *you* are worthy. When I want to look back, you redirect my eyes to the vision ahead of a redeemed life. With love, you invite me to walk in the direction of delight and peace.

FAMILY, FRIENDS, AND OTHERS

May I always look at and encourage
others with your love, Jesus.

Change of Relationship Status

*I no longer call you servants, because a servant
does not know his master's business.
Instead, I have called you friends, for everything that I
learned from my Father I have made known to you.*

JOHN 15:15

Deepening any relationship brings me joy. Some of my connections are waning, but I look forward to shifting other relationships from acquaintance status to genuine friendship. It will take the investment of being present to those others and building on what we have. I want to be able to ask hard questions and to be vulnerable with a kindred spirit.

I'm so thankful I have this kind of relationship with you, Lord. I can ask you anything and share everything. You restore my hope in connection when you walk beside me through both hardship and happy times. In your mercy, you've brought me out of the servant's house, invited me to your table, and offered me lasting friendship. You have given me the best relationship status change I could hope for.

Witnessing the Heart of Others

The LORD said to Samuel, "Do not consider his appearance or his height, for I have rejected him. The LORD does not look at the things people look at. People look at the outward appearance, but the LORD looks at the heart."

1 SAMUEL 16:7

I caught myself sizing up another person based on outward qualities rather than on who they are at heart. I've worried about what someone *might* be thinking of me. And in my family life, I've withheld my grace at times out of the desire for control.

Lord, forgive me for missing out on opportunities to connect with others and for limiting how you can use me because of judgments and restrictions I make. Give me the desire to see, hear, and know the heart of another. Release me from the concerns I have about how I'm perceived so I can be open, engaged, and fully present to your children. May you look at my heart and see it as acceptable. May it overflow with your love, Lord.

Oh, My Family!

They were at their wits' end.
Then they cried out to the LORD in their trouble,
and he brought them out of their distress.

PSALM 107:27-28

I am out of answers, Lord. This family of mine has me stressed and struggling. Some days I feel as though I'll never take a deep and peaceful breath again. I worry about their safety, happiness, faith, decisions, and unity under this roof. The evidence of their struggle is clear. Their eyes are downcast, and the words we exchange have an edge of hopelessness.

God, I long to draw them in with hugs, kind words, and grace. Show me how to love on my family with your love. Let me understand what's going on in their lives so I can lift them up in prayer and offer real help rather than criticism or control. Save us, God. Fill us with your healing breath before discouragement takes up residence.

Active Love

Whoever dwells in the shelter of the Most High
will rest in the shadow of the Almighty.
I will say of the LORD, *"He is my refuge and*
my fortress, my God, in whom I trust."

PSALM 91:1-2

My true home is bigger than my tangible shelter. It doesn't have boundaries because it's formed in your love, Lord. I'm grateful for it, and I pray to be more generous with what it offers. Create in me a spirit eager to welcome anyone and everyone to this place of acceptance, hope, protection, and mercy.

My concern expands for loved ones who bear hardship and for strangers who maneuver unsafe passages toward uncertain destinations. This worry comes from a well-meaning heart, but it isn't active love. Worry prevents me from following your call. Show me, Jesus, how to be your compassion in this world. I will pray. I will act even as I tremble. And I will gather everyone I can to join me in the godly places of physical and spiritual refuge.

CONFIDENCE

May I live confident in your
power, not my own.

Never Wasted

*Some of those present were saying indignantly to
one another, "Why this waste of perfume?"*

MARK 14:4

Lord, I'm tired of the weight of other people's opinions. I've come to second-guess the leading in my spirit. When people tell me I give too extravagantly, too modestly, or too imperfectly, it's easy to distrust my heart. I don't live boldly because I worry my offering will be judged.

I don't want my journey mapped by fear rather than by confidence. I come to you with all the faith and love Mary had when she poured perfume on your feet. I will tune out judgments of others and serve you with leaps of faith and unabashed generosity. Yes, I'll make mistakes, but you will know that the heart of this servant is focused on you.

Because I Am Loved

In him and through faith in him we may
approach God with freedom and confidence.

Ephesians 3:12

When I make strides at work and in relationships, I inevitably encounter doubt. It nudges me to hold on to insecurities rather than to step into my identity in you. But you don't leave me to be bullied by such thoughts, God; you build up the fire of faith in me. A great anticipation of purpose replaces the timidity of unbelief. Purpose and passion unfold in me each day. These are gifts you give freely, never asking me to jump through hoops or prove my abilities.

The one-word résumé I'm required to show you is *faith*. That's it. I enter this time of prayer freely and with confidence because I'm loved by the Master, I'm welcomed as friend by the Savior, and I'm approved to co-create life with the Creator.

Gaining Time

*Can any one of you by worrying add
a single hour to your life?*

MATTHEW 6:27

God, my spirit has been bound in knots because I wouldn't let go of a specific concern. It took over my conversations with my friends, my family, and my moments alone. The mental real estate it corralled was huge, but the biggest loss is the time it stole. I can't get that back.

Lord, your Word is straightforward: Can I add a single hour to my life by worrying? Absolutely not. What was I thinking? No more. I will lift my worry to your care and seek your wisdom, but I will not sacrifice my life to fretting. This is how I add time to my life and life to my time, Lord. You've told me all along. I can't wait to see how you'll use me as I walk in grace with confidence.

Look!

~

See! The winter is past; the rains are over and gone.

SONG OF SOLOMON 2:11

I am so grateful, God. You're turning me in the direction of hope. When I dwell on the past, trying to recast my regrettable moments in a better light, it's more about sparing my pride than about preparing for purpose. You tell me this in the early hours of the morning when I can't sleep. And you tell me to look toward what comes after the storms or the barren winter.

I don't want to become rooted in my old story. I want to grow toward my new one. You free me to do this with simple directions: *Look! See!* Today I believe the rains are over and gone. The sun is warming the earth I walk on, and the light of your love is highlighting the way forward.

JOY

May I set my course
toward your joy, Jesus.

Bring Me Joy

When anxiety was great within me,
your consolation brought me joy.

PSALM 94:19

Jesus, the peace you've provided my spirit is transforming. How great was the anxiety that ruled my heart before, when I couldn't make a good decision or take steps of faith. It's easy to become singular in my focus to figure out my work and my relationships on my own. Why was I ever surprised when I was left dissatisfied and weary in my belief?

Your comfort and understanding breathe restoration into my soul and bones. A deep and true joy is within me now when I wake up and start another 24-hour segment of this life. Gone is the oppressing weight of anticipating trouble. You bring me joy and the excitement of possibility.

Love Parade

> *Thanks be to God, who in Christ always leads us in triumphal procession, and through us spreads the fragrance of the knowledge of him everywhere.*
>
> 2 CORINTHIANS 2:14 ESV

'’ve never been one to rush to the front of a crowd to see a parade go by. I might peek around people to catch a glimpse of who or what is passing, but I don't make much effort. It's not my thing.

You know this about me, Lord. That's why you've grabbed my hand and pulled me into the procession. This is a time to participate in spreading the fragrance of who you are. Those on the sidelines want your love, and they cheer when your compassion is passed out freely. You hold my hand as we walk, and you reach for others to step in cadence beside us. This isn't an exclusive parade. You ask me and others to keep spreading your joy and proclaiming your love.

Worth Repeating

〜

Rejoice in the Lord always. I will say it again: Rejoice!
PHILIPPIANS 4:4

Lord, often my focus settles on what's going wrong while I let my blessings fade to the background. This isn't how I want to experience this one life, so I will give my time and attention to highlighting what is good and right. You instill wisdom in my heart in the middle of tough decisions. You have showered me with life-giving conversations with others. You've nudged me forward or held me back at the right time. Your peace has filled me when there were no words to ease my worry. The list grows each time I give thought to how I can trust your presence.

In this moment and in every moment, I can rejoice in knowing you and in being your child. I will say it again: Rejoice! This is how I keep your blessings in view, gracious God.

My Strength

*Don't be dejected and sad, for the joy
of the LORD is your strength!*

NEHEMIAH 8:10 NLT

Some harsh words came my way from someone I know. Maybe they weren't meant to hurt me or to cause me to question my value, but still, I've let those words burrow deep into my heart. My hope is to replace them with your Word. That isn't easy to do. I've tried before only to return to believing lies and even basing my choices on them.

Help me to see my value in you. Instead of trying to hold up the weight of other people's expectations, I long to lean on you. My joy comes when I trust in your strength and make it the foundation I stand on. In my weakness I put my faith in another's perspective. In your strength my faith is never misplaced.

WANT

May my longing
be filled by you.

Overflowing

*In the midst of a very severe trial,
their overflowing joy and their extreme
poverty welled up in rich generosity.*

2 Corinthians 8:2

In times of hardship, I recalculate and plan to ensure I'll have what I believe I need or what my family needs. I search high and low for ways to receive. But, God, you meet me in the trial and show me this is a season to give. With encouragement and opportunities to do good, you unveil the needs of others in and beyond my circle.

I keep thinking the flow of joy and pain or wealth and poverty is an either/or force. I instinctively clench my hand and heart to keep what little I have. But you release my grip and reveal how an open hand and heart are better able to receive *and* give of your blessings. My fear is washed away by overflowing joy as you lead me to the riches of your generosity.

Giving from Little or from a Lot

They all gave out of their wealth;
but she, out of her poverty,
put in everything—all she had to live on.

MARK 12:44

What am I scared of? Lord, you know my heart and I know the generosity of yours, so why does the topic of money and future provision send me reeling? My thoughts land on worst-case scenarios, including the possibility of not being able to help those around me—both those who depend on me and those placed on my heart to support in some way. I think if I have little, I'll be able to give only little. This is such faulty thinking, because I'm not the provider; you are!

God, grant me your deep peace. I don't have to worry about my future or my future giving. Your call to my heart will be the same in plenty or in poverty: to keep sharing of my money, time, and journey, and of your love, which is replenished and overflowing in every season.

So Many Good Things

*I will bless her with abundant provisions;
her poor, I will satisfy with food.*

PSALM 132:15

Generous Lord, you bless me and then bless me again. You've provided for my every need over the years. Even when I didn't know *what* I needed, you set in motion everything required to fill my heart, body, and mind with so many good things. You give grace to the sinner. You extend mercy to the unjust. You heal the hurting with the balm of love. You stay with the wanderer. And you bless me in both days of surplus and in days of want.

I'm grateful the people I love are in your care. When I'm unsure what they need to live in faith and wholeness, you set in motion what will fill them. They are given their daily bread physically and spiritually because you're the gracious provider. I am humbled by God things.

Giving Up

Your fasting ends in quarreling and strife,
and in striking each other with wicked fists.
You cannot fast as you do today
and expect your voice to be heard on high.

ISAIAH 58: 4

God, my deep sense of lack comes because I'm starved for your love. I fast from faith rather than from food or distraction. I look at my neighbors and wish for their life. I become jealous over my friends' accomplishments when I compare them to my setbacks. My mind spins, wondering how I can be filled up with what isn't even meant for me. I live motivated by perceived lack even though you provide all I'll ever need for my journey.

Forgive me, Jesus, for starving myself spiritually. May you hear my voice today declare that it is you I crave. May all my hungers lead me to be fed by your mercies.

REFRESHMENT

May I come to your well to
have my thirst quenched.

In Your Garden

They will still bear fruit in old age,
they will stay fresh and green.

PSALM 92:14

Refresh me, God. A trouble has taxed my mind and spirit, and I'm tired. I wait anxiously for old aspects of my life to fall away and for new sprigs of hope to take their place. Show me the signs of renewal and resurrection. In the past, I haven't always welcomed the pruning process. Out of fear, I resisted your leading just so I could keep a job or a relationship the same. But now I'm far more afraid of never changing or bearing new fruit.

Resurrect my creativity and energy, Lord. Fill my dreams with vibrant images and my mind with engaging ideas. I want to be refreshed from the inside out. Grow in me the green, new shoots of spiritual awakening. I long to be a new creation.

Water Supply

Spring up, O well! Sing about it.
NUMBERS 21:17

'm parched. The terrain of my days has been dry and lifeless. The starkness of my desert season has skewed my perspective. When I see others rejoicing about a new opportunity or a dream that has come to fruition, my throat tightens in response. My lack of satisfaction is making me cynical. Lord, I don't want to be focused on what I don't have; I want to wait with contentment and gratitude for your care.

You don't forget your children. You release the long-awaited well to spring forth and sate my soul. I run through the cool waters and lift my voice to praise you for such needed refreshment. May I serve others from this place of joy and delight in their delight without holding back.

Rest Stop

He refreshes my soul. He guides me along
the right paths for his name's sake.

PSALM 23:3

I've been looking ahead, squinting to see what my life and my various choices will throw onto my path. I get anxious wondering how you'll usher me from pain to joy if these possible events occur down the road. It amazes me that I still do this, even though I know I'm missing out on your presence right here, right now. You are guiding me in the circumstance I face today. I can rest in the truth that you'll remain even when my situations—good or difficult—happen years from now.

I'll take in some deep breaths. I'll stretch my faith by entrusting to you those future possibilities. You refresh my spirit and my joy as you ask me to simply and boldly walk the portion of path right in front of me...*with* you.

Gulp

I will refresh the weary and satisfy the faint.
JEREMIAH 31:25

I'm drinking in every ounce of your refreshment, God. You sate my spirit with promises and ease my heartache with the balm of blessing. I thought this would be a season of only parched want, but your love comes to me in waves of affection from within and from others you lead to be your voice or loving arms.

The difficulty that's consumed my thoughts releases when I step from behind the shelter I created to protect myself from possible hurt. It's scary to be exposed to the elements of the world, but now I can gulp in your rained-down-on-me love. I can be blessed by each offering of help, each sincere inquiry about how I'm doing, and each moment of acceptance or prayer with a soul friend.

SUCCESS

May I turn any fret about failure
into a reason to trust you.

Morning Meeting

*Be ready in the morning, and then
come up on Mount Sinai.
Present yourself to me there on top of the mountain.*

EXODUS 34:2

God, you witness me at my disheveled worst. I wake up feeling rumpled inside and out from unresolved needs and pressing worries. My spirit doesn't feel presentable for a holy encounter. But you summon me to come to you. Oh, God, how do you love me like you do?

I don't need to overcome the rugged cliffs of a mountain to reach you, because every place can be holy in your presence. I need to overcome the mental blocks and the fears that might keep me lying in bed, unable to face the day. I don't need to unravel my worries or smooth out my rough places. I need only to show up—wholly messy, wholly me, with holy you.

Sky Full of Promise

*I will surely bless you and make your descendants
as numerous as the stars in the sky and as the sand
on the seashore...because you have obeyed me.*

GENESIS 22:17-18

I am unprepared for this life thing. It isn't easy to wake up to the unknowns and then walk through them toward success. And what is success, anyway? I don't know which way to turn to invest my time. Give me a sense of your guidance, God.

I feel you place your hand on my shoulder and point me in the direction I should go. You aren't angry when I don't measure up to the goal; you bless me when I'm mindful of how to obey you. Show me how to be righteous. Open my eyes to the path prepared for me so I can honor you with my steps, choices, prayers, hopes, objectives, intentions, and pursuits. I long to see your promises fulfilled as you set in motion blessings as abundant as the stars.

Just Not That

*When the young man heard this, he went
away sad, because he had great wealth.*

MATTHEW 19:22

What do I hold on to, God, that comes between me and the abundant life you offer? Like the young rich man who wanted to know how to enter your kingdom, I strive to keep your commandments. I know in my heart who you are and why I want to be with you forever. And how often I am also like him when he shakes his head and walks away because you've asked for complete surrender of the one thing that's becoming so important that it clouds the eyes of the soul. Do I draw the line at my success? My comfort?

What do I give my passion and worried attention to that distracts me from communion with you? Show me where I misplace my faith. Give me the courage to surrender all.

Complete Victory

*Consider it pure joy, my brothers and sisters,
whenever you face trials of many kinds, because
you know that the testing of your faith produces
perseverance...Let perseverance finish its work
so that you may be mature and complete.*

JAMES 1:2-4

This is not how I envisioned claiming joy, God. Some hard situations are in my home and in my life. I feel the weight of failure more often than the levity and victory of success. I gather worries and store them rather than release them for your transformation. Maybe I'm resistant to learning from trials because that means I must acknowledge their existence.

God, help me say yes to the fruit of perseverance you're birthing in my current trials. Give me a willingness to see my struggles without the need to apologize for or deny them. I want to be a witness to all you're doing in my spirit. I pray to be a witness to the lasting, satisfying joy you shape before my open eyes.

HOPE

May today's discouragement be a
doorway to your shelter of hope.

A Promise Realized

*After waiting patiently, Abraham
received what was promised.*

HEBREWS 6:15

God, I'm in that dark place of uncertainty. The light of what is known has dimmed, and I'm looking at shadows and silhouettes as I pace. It's just been one of those weeks, when small setbacks seem bigger, heavier, and riskier than they probably are.

I must rest my mind on what's real. You have taught me to be still. To wait for your light and your love to infuse these times. I don't know what my finances will look like next month or how a recent conflict will be resolved, but I do know you honor your promises. You illuminate every dark corner, and you show me that those silhouettes are not of obstacles; they are of your future promises to be fulfilled.

Fulfilled Heart

*I consider my life worth nothing to me;
my only aim is to finish the race
and complete the task the Lord Jesus has given me—
the task of testifying to the good news of God's grace.*

ACTS 20:24

How will I use the breath you give me? This is the question I want to—*need* to—ask every morning upon rising. Give me wisdom to know how to move forward in the tasks for each day that aren't ordinary to-do list qualifiers but to-be invitations. To be present for others. To be open to the quirky twists a day can take. To be willing to accept a new version of what my race might look like.

Most of all, Lord, help me set aside my agenda of worries so my words don't rise from an anxious heart. Instead let them rise on your breath in me as I speak of your grace and fulfill your heart for others.

You

*LORD, there is no one like you to help
the powerless against the mighty.*

2 CHRONICLES 14:11

The broken world is searching. Oh, how we ache to believe there is someone who will not abandon us. Who will help the one who is downcast? Who will lead the one struggling to take a single step? Who reaches down into the pit where the fallen reside in darkness? Who will champion us in our times of disappointment and sorrow?

My spirit knows the answer: you, God. You stand up against the mighty and merciless, and you never forsake the one in need. Grant me humility to become a helper, leader, rescuer, and companion. I want to be a hopeful child of the One who champions the powerless, the fulfiller of promises, the giver of courage.

Cleared for Takeoff

*I will turn all my mountains into roads,
and my highways will be raised up.*

ISAIAH 49:11

Not long ago, I was staring down mountains. The thought of pursuing the path I trusted was from you was daunting. Getting a running start seemed futile. I felt foolish stating my intention to rush forward to make it over the peaks that rose in front of me. But I vowed to trust you for all things. So today I'm going for it. Whatever I see ahead that strikes concern in me is insurmountable only if I attempt to overcome it in my own power.

I'm surrendering to your will, Lord. That mountain ahead? It's nothing to you. You not only turn it into a road; you transform it into a runway and tell me to fly in the direction of every dream you hold for me.

SECURITY

May I trade my insecurity and
doubt for your assurance, Lord.

Come What May

When you pass through the waters,
I will be with you; and when you pass through
the rivers, they will not sweep over you. When
you walk through the fire, you will not be
burned; the flames will not set you ablaze.

ISAIAH 43:2

Do my prayers change much over the years, Lord? Maybe it's just my perspective, but it seems like I lift up the same concerns and fears over and over. This isn't because you don't answer my prayers; it's because I choose to rest into the worries more than I press into my belief.

Yet no matter what I encounter, you are with me. No crowded room, desolate hiking trail, or hospital waiting room can separate me from your care and protection. I'm emboldened to journey into my tomorrows with comfort in this truth. What is there to fear if I know I can lean into your strength? Infuse me with faith and courage, Lord. I will trust you come what may.

Again, I Will Have Peace

*I will surely save you out of a distant place,
your descendants from the land of their exile.
Jacob will again have peace and security,
and no one will make him afraid.*

JEREMIAH 30:10

Sometimes I've felt in exile—cast away from the life I thought you were calling me to, God. I wonder if I'm too far from the purpose you called me to.

But I know you're here with me. With relief I settle into your presence. I sense your invitation to lay down my worries and stay for eternity. I no longer have a consuming fear that I missed all the signs pointing out the right direction. You have saved me and shown me what it is to remain in you and live from your Spirit. Again, I will have peace. The questions and the turns won't make me afraid. There isn't a place I can travel by thought or by foot that will take me away from the homeland of your heart.

All My Ways

*He will command his angels concerning
you to guard you in all your ways.*

PSALM 91:11

Lord, I'm grateful for your care and protection. I've felt it often and witnessed the ways you are with me. When I can't sleep, you give me a word of peace. And on those days when worries speak louder than my faith, I recall times when you've provided for me or seen me through a difficulty. I believe in the doings of your unseen hand. I've heard you speak truth to me through times of decision. Strangers have extended kindness to me only minutes after I felt the pang of loneliness.

Give me spiritual sight to notice and appreciate when you guide my next step or pull me back from error with wisdom and direction. Guard my ways, dear Lord, and let my days be proof of your power at work.

Brought to Safety

*We went through fire and water, but you
brought us to a place of abundance.*

PSALM 66:12

Both natural and personal disasters play out in the
news and online daily. Those tragedies and pending losses are also part of my internal life. When my
spirit is on fire with doubt or my heart is flooded with
grief, my response is the same: I want control. I can't
bear to have what I care about burn to the ground or
wash away.

But you are showing me that order and healing will
come later. My insistence to find what I care about
unmarred among the cinder and debris isn't realistic—
or of faith. Faith anticipates more. From the rubble,
you will create something new and abundant. This is
the promise you whisper when you pull your children
from the wreckage and draw us into your safe embrace.

PURPOSE

May I walk in the holy way of
your purpose for me, Creator.

The Safety of Your Shore

*The rest were to get there on planks
or on other pieces of the ship.
In this way everyone reached land safely.*

ACTS 27:44

God, I feel at sea and far from purpose. In one moment, I strongly sense a course to follow. In the next moment, I question that course, and I'm more certain about a pursuit in the opposite direction. I'm living in the aftermath of waves caused by change and doubts, both mine and those of people in my life.

Today is the day I will grab onto a piece of debris that floats past me. It will be the life raft I need to turn around and get back to you. I'm kicking my legs and splashing my way back to your shore. My spirit knows how to do this even without the help of starlight, because you've never moved. You've remained there in anticipation of my safe return.

Tender Words

*I am now going to allure her; I will lead her
into the wilderness and speak tenderly to her.
There I will give her back her vineyards, and
will make the Valley of Achor a door of hope.*

HOSEA 2:14-15

God, you speak to my soul like no other. Your tenderness moves me and allows me to let down my guard—the one I build as a safety barrier between me and others or even between my spirit and my negative thoughts. The promises you whisper to me are of redemption and restoration. The past few years I've felt as though I've gone backward rather than made progress in my purpose. I sense I'm left behind as others rise in their calling and show evidence of growth.

Then I hear your voice. You have not forgotten me or the ways you want to lead me. You will show me the landscape of purpose and restore to me the hope I had before this season of doubt.

This Land Is My Land

I will give you every place where you set your foot.

JOSHUA 1:3

God, your grace has pulled me out of the trenches created by long-treaded frets. For years I didn't fully believe I could walk on the holy ground of purpose. Then you saved me from disbelief. Through your love and mercy, I am made worthy to stand on the firm ground of your hope for me.

I grieve how much time I wasted believing everything had to be perfect first, that I had to reach a level of achievement before you would see me as a child to call into purpose. You reassure me that even that time can be redeemed. Everywhere I go, you point to the place I stand and reaffirm that it's ground upon which your purpose for me can be built.

Free

When you walk, your steps will not be hampered;
when you run, you will not stumble.

PROVERBS 4:12

Lord, you have set me free. When my pursuit of a noble calling is slowed by the unexpected needs of my family, you're not holding me back. When the inspired ideas that motivated me toward dreams from you hit the snags of reality and logistics, you set me free. As I wonder if it's too late to ever enter the land of purpose, you set me free.

My mind is what binds me and distracts me, because tangents can become more comfortable than worries. When I'm close to giving up, my spirit cries out to you and echoes back to me the promises you've made. Lord, you do not hinder this child of yours. You've set me free to run in your purpose.

FAITHFULNESS

May I open my eyes to see, believe,
and follow your faithfulness.

All You Do

The LORD is righteous in all his ways
and faithful in all he does.

PSALM 145:17

Such goodness flows through my journey because of you, God. The busy pace with which I maneuver through time and work and the world doesn't allow the wonder to sink in, and that's a shame. When I pause to examine the gifts I encounter in a 24-hour slice of lifetime, I'm in awe. God, you provide so much, and you are faithful in every way.

What would I be without your nudges to show compassion to others or your display of kindness to me through friends? How would I withstand tough news and uncertain tomorrows if not for the certainty I have that you hear my every prayer—even the ones that don't make it past my trembling lips? Your goodness amazes me. May I always live and give as one who is grateful that you are faithful.

Getting There

*The LORD will vindicate me; your love, LORD, endures
forever—do not abandon the works of your hands.*

PSALM 138:8

Please, Lord. Never quit shaping me into the person
you dreamed into being, formed in the womb, and
guided up to this very second. Forgive me for becoming discouraged or disappointed over my daily life and
the mundane moments.

Deep in my spirit, the well of your mercy nourishes
me and revives my hope. I will get there. In your vindication and strength, I will get to my purpose. And I will
live from a deeper understanding of each relationship,
conversation, and decision. The offerings of your grace
will continue your work in me—the work of your very
hands. My missteps won't direct my calling, because
you redeem all my fragile humanness in your divine
love. I am moved by your steadfast attention and presence. You've never given up on me.

The Foiled Getaway

That day when evening came, he said to his disciples, "Let us go over to the other side."

MARK 4:35

Lord, I love the story of when you requested a getaway to the other side of the lake for respite from the crowds. The great need around you sparked the great need within you for restoration. Then when you fell asleep in the boat, the winds came. The disciples awakened you to soothe their worries as well as the waves. The small faith of your followers was disappointing. Still, you calmed the storm. Even in your fatigue and frustration, Jesus, you showed them compassion.

Let me find my way to such love. When the needs of others interfere with my chances to get away and be restored, give me a heart that offers them peace. Show me what it looks like to be faithful when all my plans are washed away.

Establish Faithfulness

May the favor of the Lord our God rest on us;
establish the work of our hands for us—
yes, establish the work of our hands.

PSALM 90:17

A single thread of worry seems to be woven throughout the history of my days. I question whether I'm doing what's meaningful and true for this one life I have. Whatever number of years and days I'll be given, I long for them to be fruitful. Do I have an impact, Lord? Have I expressed your love to others? What is the work of my hands and spirit to be, God?

Bless me with this insight and with the courage to honor the answer. I'm eager to break that thread of worry so I can instead weave together strands of a story about your favor and my faithfulness.

HEALING

May I confess my brokenness to receive
your mending and redemption.

The Repair of My Despair

*We were under great pressure, far beyond our
ability to endure, so that we despaired of life itself.
Indeed, we felt we had received the sentence of
death. But this happened that we might not rely
on ourselves but on God, who raises the dead.*

2 Corinthians 1:8-9

This body my soul wears has its struggles, but forgive me for the moments when I fault it. This physical self that experiences pain is an amazing creation; I know this.

Yet I despair at the thought of bolstering the energy to figure out life. Temporary setbacks are familiar, and I adjust. It's the longer journey, Lord, that spins webs of worry in my mind. As unnerving as unknowns are, they lead to a certainty: I don't have the power to reset my body or the time set in motion the moment I was born. I'm not the one who restores body and soul. The light of truth here is that I'm completely dependent upon you. Despair will not endure in divine hands that repair and resurrect their creation.

Rich Harvest of Hardship

*It is because God has made me fruitful
in the land of my suffering.*

GENESIS 41:52

I would never have dreamed such gifts would grow from a past season of suffering. I wouldn't have believed it even if someone had sat me down and explained how your grace transforms bitter loss into expanded capacity for compassion, and pain-occupied seasons into land fertile for awareness and wisdom.

Words of potential joy in the middle of distress can spark a light of hope, but they can also cause deeper pain. Jesus, your power to redeem our brokenness seems too good to be true. But I know it to *be* true. When it's difficult to place my feet on the floor and start my day, I will recall that I am stepping on fruitful land.

Show Me

*Ask the LORD your God for a sign, whether in
the deepest depths or in the highest heights.*

ISAIAH 7:11

I want to stay under the covers. I'm barely noticing life happening around me, so why should I be out among the living? I don't comprehend what people say to me. I know they're offering me encouragements, but their sentences sound garbled. They're speaking in a code I'm much too tired to decipher.

As much as I want to deny it, I'm in the deepest depths, God. I worry that soon I won't be able to see your sky. Show me a sign. I need confirmation that I'm not forgotten, that I'm still in your care. It feels good to ask. I know your love will shine like a flare. I can enter a bleak day less lonely and unafraid that my hurt will swallow me whole.

When I Was Wronged

Love covers over all wrongs.

PROVERBS 10:12

God, you have watched over me since before I was born. When I was hurt intentionally or unknowingly, you witnessed it. You shed light on it. And you provided me with comfort and truth so I wouldn't hold more tightly to the hurt than to the healing. Even when I didn't know you as I do now, I felt your provision. Your love covered me and the wrongs of others. Broken trust can lead to broken hearts, but you mend the spirits of your children. You see our wounds and don't let them become who we are.

I'm thankful I can rest in the certainty of your love. When I worry about being wronged again, you remind me to trust in you as my ever-present protector and shepherd.

ACCEPTANCE

May I live and act from my
worthiness as your child.

Good as Gold

*He knows the way that I take; when he has
tested me, I will come forth as gold.*

JOB 23:10

God, when I look at life through my hazy window of worry, I set up a bad-versus-good comparison. If I'm living the bad, I long for the good as though the two experiences are unrelated. When I look at my problem through your eternal view, I see that we're moving toward good *because* of this journey. As gold is refined through heat and fire, my spiritual growth is refined through the intensity and discomfort of difficulties. They're gifts. This is when I draw closer to you and deepen my faith. I prepare to recognize goodness.

Instead of giving energy toward worrying about or wishing away this rough path, I will walk it with gratitude. I will have hope for the day I come forth as gold.

Spiritual Schooling

*It was good for me to be afflicted so
that I might learn your decrees.*

PSALM 119:71

I get it, Lord. The school of faith is in session even if I didn't hear the bell ring. I've wanted to avoid learning in this season because life is sort of hard. I have a lot on my mind, and I wonder how I can possibly fill it with more information. How can you expect this of me?

But you tell me to put down my hand, that there will be time for questions later. Now you want to speak to me in my affliction, my angst. You're filling my spirit with truth and love and an acceptance so mighty it makes me sit upright. My mind will catch up later. Right now you're pouring your decrees into the well of my being so I will forever be taught the truth of my worthiness.

Me? Really?

The LORD longs to be gracious to you;
therefore he will rise up to show you compassion.

ISAIAH 30:18

Your graciousness covers and completes me. It washes away the uncertainty I felt in a situation fraught with unknowns and that magnified my insecurities. Like an animal who goes off into the woods to tend to its wounds, I distanced myself from help. Such stubbornness can be fatal, if not for the rush of your love that overpowers my resistance and pride.

You, the creator of the physical and spiritual heart, long to be gracious to me. I let this sink in along with your peace, which filters and sifts through obstinance and loneliness. It reaches the core of me. You gather me up. In your compassion, you accept my wounds and flaws one by one and heal me toward wholeness.

Bearing Together

I am the vine; you are the branches.
If you remain in me and I in you,
you will bear much fruit.

JOHN 15:5

Lord, my eye has been on the prize for many years, and I hoped the results of my labor would be praised as fruitful and profound. At times I've felt that I've achieved success. But the prize I have my eye on seems to change. So does my sense of worth and accomplishment. How did I get so far from the roots of my purpose in you?

The greatest treasures my life produces won't be those I gain on my own or for my honor. When I join with you and your steadfast love and spirit remain in me, I will bear the richest fruit. The kind of fruit that feeds those who are spiritually and physically hungry. Together, we bear fruit prized as a blessing.

PRAISE

May I proclaim your strength
and mercy at all times.

Ongoing Praise

*Through Jesus, therefore, let us continually
offer to God a sacrifice of praise—
the fruit of lips that openly profess his name.*

HEBREWS 13:15

Let my lips speak your holy name, God, and may my life be an act of praise. I'm blessed in many ways, and I always have been. Troubles come with the rising of the sun, and many are resolved before the moon makes its showing. Problems don't disappear because I have faith, but they do fade to the background when I'm offering a sacrifice of adoration and worship.

I pray my affection for you is evident in the way I talk of you and your grace. May others know of your faithfulness through my proclamations as well as by the peace I have and that I choose when worry tempts me to withhold gratitude. Give me a heart that will continually praise you, Jesus, in every circumstance.

For the Benefit of Others

*So they took away the stone. Then
Jesus looked up and said,
"Father, I thank you that you have heard me.
I knew that you always hear me, but I said
this for the benefit of the people standing here,
that they may believe that you sent me."*

JOHN 11:41-42

Jesus, your fierce love for people was revealed through your grief and compassion even before your crucifixion. When your friend Lazarus died, you sought the power of the Father to raise him from the dead. Your heart compelled you to action and prayer on behalf of a child of God. And you proclaimed his mercy so that everyone around you would know of God's faithfulness.

May I live this way too. Let me sing and shout my praises even before the dying parts of my faith and purpose are resurrected. I want my journey of trust to benefit others and remind them that they, too, are always heard by the Father in shadows of heartache.

Abundant Wonders

Many, LORD my God, are the wonders you have done,
the things you planned for us.
None can compare with you; were I to speak and tell
of your deeds, they would be too many to declare.

PSALM 40:5

Lord, my mind sifts through potential worries with a strange sense of productivity and comfort. You have created countless wonders for your children, and so many good plans are in the making. Why aren't my mind and heart fixed on *these*?

Acts of your love are plentiful, and if I watch for them as I go about my day, I'll witness them. Every one of your children is special, worthy, and eager to be heard and hugged. Creation showcases your brilliance and your desire to inspire and delight. I might not be able to declare all your deeds and miracles, but Lord, let me become someone who at least tries!

Just Look at All This

*He who did not spare his own Son, but gave
him up for us all—how will he not also, along
with him, graciously give us all things?*

ROMANS 8:32

Thank you, God, for your perfect provision. If I start a day intending to gather and point out the gifts you've prepared, I end that day comforted by your generosity. I want to show others the ways you are present and active. So many people believe you're an elusive deity, a universal truth that never becomes a personal Messiah.

Forgive me when I direct attention to the fear-tinged unknowns instead of highlighting all the knowns that come from you. How much better would be my life offering to you and your children (not to mention to my entire human experience) if I used my voice to praise you for each gift rather than to magnify each fret. "Look at all this. It's from the Lord." It's that easy.

FEAR

May I stand in your light,
which dispels all fear.

Toward You

*Do not be afraid, Daniel. Since the first day that
you set your mind to gain understanding and to
humble yourself before your God, your words were
heard, and I have come in response to them.*

DANIEL 10:12

I want to know you, God. I hunger to understand you and your love. Every truth I absorb delivers me to a state of awe and worship. Who am I, but a person struggling to unwind the worries that plague my mind and grip my heart? Release me from the pattern of thinking negatively when so much joy and greatness exist to captivate my attention.

In my frailty, I'll turn all of me—body, mind, soul—toward you for help. I'll lift my praise and the chaos of my confusion too. You sift through and hear every word. In the mix of laments about my ordinary life or cries about the trials that single me out, you focus on the underlying message that exists always: I need you. Come to me, Lord.

S.O.S.

*A furious squall came up, and the waves broke
over the boat, so that it was nearly swamped.*

MARK 4:37

Out of nowhere, the storm waves rise above me. I'm caught by surprise because I believed my avoidance of trouble was working. For months I tossed overboard any emotion that threatened to rock this boat sailing for status quo. Now that same debris surfaces with a force too powerful for my flimsy flotation device of denial. In fear, I cry out to you from the depths of my soul: *Savior. Oh, Savior.* You pluck me from the dark waters and take me to the dry land of truth and your mercy shores.

I'm sorry I waited until the point of distress, Lord, but here I am—drenched, stripped of my belongings and myths, a castaway from the world...and forever grateful.

Is It Just Me?

*We will not fear, though the earth give way and
the mountains fall into the heart of the sea.*

PSALM 46:2

Troubles clamor in my spirit, God. Fear about a decision shakes my core and forms cracks in the ground beneath me. I fixate on potential errors and then foresee the disaster of messing up the purpose you have for me. Yet you have created a certain foundation that never crumbles—the one made of your love and righteousness.

Is it just me? No. Never. It's me and you. My frailty becomes the fertile landscape to plant your strength. My considerable insecurity in walking in a difficult direction will become a showcase for my security in you. Thankfully, the only thing that falls away is my unwillingness to trust you completely to transform my fault lines into your lifelines.

No Fear

There is no fear in love. But perfect love drives out fear.

1 JOHN 4:18

Fear has stolen so much from me. But your love has driven away dread and replaced it with new life and hope. You don't cast me away when I timidly enter your presence, afraid that you are tired of me and my meager efforts. Instead you embrace me and cast away my worries. You leave me empowered and unburdened to walk in the purpose you guide me to.

I feel the power of your mercy in my spirit, and I see its gifts when goodness rises out of my seasons of struggle. Where there was distance, now there is intimacy. Where there was regret, now there is relief. Your perfect love has saved me.

FUTURE

May I turn my feet and my heart
toward your future for me.

Where Are We Going?

*He makes me lie down in green pastures,
he leads me beside quiet waters,
he refreshes my soul.*

PSALM 23:2-3

God, where are you taking me? I'm trying to see around the bend to glimpse the future hope you have for me. I need to believe goodness is up ahead. I worry I've stepped over or around my blessing of purpose.

But where I'm going is not as important as who I'm going with—you. And you calm my concerns with each step forward. My eyes adjust to see your promises clearly. At your encouragement, I lie down to rest. Questions about the what and how of my future fade as the sound of quiet waters flows in place of the worries. My hope is refreshed, restored.

Inherited Faith

*By faith Abraham, when called to go to a place he
would later receive as his inheritance,
obeyed and went, even though he did
not know where he was going.*

HEBREWS 11:8

No sound investments come from man—not truly. When I think I have security in my future because of human decisions and abilities to forecast tomorrow and the day after that, I'm fooling myself. People look quizzically at faith and call it blind and unsubstantiated. But I know that in faith is an inheritance that puts any earthly wealth to shame. The future you've created and prepared for me as your heir is what I walk toward with hope.

God, grant me peace when my home, money, or job doesn't fulfill the expectations I have assigned to it. None of those are meant to do that, but your love is. I can follow you, Father, with certainty.

The Things You Know

*All the days ordained for me were written in
your book before one of them came to be.*

PSALM 139:16

Lord, what you know but I don't know could fill a book (and much of it has!). What you know can also fill my spirit and my life if I'll let it. But I desire control. I want to have certainty about what a person will do, how I will get from A to B, where I'll find what I'm looking for, and what to expect next. But I'm not meant to have these details; they're the mysterious unfolding parts of my experience you alone foresee.

You invite me to trust you with my every need. My eyes are open now, Lord, and so is my heart. My life is an open book—to be filled with the future adventures, losses, joys, encounters, and wonders you've written for me to live out with faith.

Belief in Blessings

*The LORD blessed the latter part of Job's
life more than the former part.*

JOB 42:12

Someone asked if I thought my best times were behind me, Lord. At first, this depressed me. What if this were true? But then I thought about your power and plan, and my spirit was lifted. Your sweet mercies aren't contained to one season of a person's journey. In so many ways, I'm only beginning to walk a faith-empowered life, and I'm excited about the paths you point me toward.

Don't let me play it safe. Please. I want to follow you with joy into the mystery of "next." I'll start praying with a belief in blessings to come. I'll keep watch for all the gifts you place in my days. And I'll celebrate the color, beauty, and wonder of these treasures that will only become more vivid in time—just like my hope in you.

GUIDANCE

May my worries be quelled so I
can listen for your leading.

Ready to Listen

*Whether you turn to the right or to the left,
your ears will hear a voice behind you saying,
"This is the way; walk in it."*

ISAIAH 30:21

I've wandered for some time, trying to use my own sense of direction and maps drawn by humans. Now I imagine sitting on a bench by a physical intersection of country roads, drinking the last drop of water and shaking my head. This is it? I ask. This time I keep still, waiting for an answer.

My weariness causes my mental chatter to cease. Finally, I hear your voice. Has it been there all along? I'm humbled and slightly embarrassed that I've asked and asked for guidance in such a storm of words and emotions that I forgot to make space to *listen*. Your loving instruction is clear: *This is the way; walk in it.* I hear you, Lord. I forget my thirst and stand up with renewed energy. I know the way to go.

In the Palm of God's Hand

Do not fear, for I am with you;
do not be dismayed, for I am your God.
I will strengthen you and help you; I will
uphold you with my righteous right hand.

ISAIAH 41:10

I look back over my harder months and notice how often I seek help where I'll never find it. Lord, I go to the same source, person, or line of thought countless times and come away frustrated because I don't receive what I need. Family and friends are trying to find their way through trials just as I am. Give me the strength to release them from the burden of being my only help.

You are my help. I rest in your palm to know the feeling of strength beneath me. You may lead me to others for encouragement and insight, or you might call me to encourage another. Either way, you are my God and my guide. I'm upheld by your righteous right hand. This is the starting place of all peace.

Overcoming

This is love for God: to keep his commands.
And his commands are not burdensome,
for everyone born of God overcomes the world.

1 John 5:3-4

I awakened with a worry on my mind. My first response was to make a plan toward resolution. On days like this, I think living in my own power is less burdensome than trusting your commands. But your commands aren't weighty shackles; they're the key to my release from circular thinking and self-made traps. Following you is not my punishment but my privilege. It's my way to a path of freedom and availability.

With trust, I take this morning's concern to your presence and ask, seek, and knock. I put my feet on the floor, eager to move in your commands toward wholeness. This is loving you. This is overcoming the world.

Teacher! Teacher!

I am the LORD your God,
who teaches you what is best for you,
who directs you in the way you should go.

ISAIAH 48:17

Like a new student hoping to be accepted by her teacher, I raise my hand often and ask questions looking for wisdom and assurances. The false teachers who've accompanied me for legs of my journey have guided my spirit with worry and woe, but now I'm released from lies and accepted as a student of yours forevermore.

When I don't get the answer right, you are gentle with your correction. You never leave me without the hope of an answer, because you lovingly teach what is best for me—even when that best is to wait on your calling. I need not be fearful. The perfect score comes at the end of my days. Right now, I'm here to learn, grow, and become a student of your grace.

COMPASSION

May I run to your embrace
of unconditional love.

Expand My Heart

*Be kind and compassionate to one another,
forgiving each other,
just as in Christ God forgave you.*

EPHESIANS 4:32

Lately, I'm bumping up against my rough edges. In places of the heart that used to be open and compassionate, I've allowed borders and restrictions to rise.

Give me your compassion, God, for me and for others. Soften and expand my heart so that my spirit never draws a line that keeps me from truly seeing and caring for another person in the way you would lead me. Give me your compassion for each person I encounter. And give me the desire and ability to forgive those in my life against whom I've fostered grudges or kept at a distance for any number of reasons. I want a heart that has no rough edges and can freely share the great love you offer all of your creation.

A Merciful King

The Almighty is beyond our reach and exalted in power;
in his justice and great righteousness, he does not oppress.

JOB 37:23

I enter the gates of your presence with wonder, Lord. I speak in a hushed tone and walk with a light step toward you, my King. I'm encountering your royal stature and power, and it's so humbling. You can do all things, yet you choose to spend time with me.

Nothing takes place in your kingdom without your knowledge, and yet you never throw my sins in my face or cast me away from your presence because of my unfaithful heart. Instead you reign with mercy and invite me to sit with you and to have my heart filled, soothed with your grace. I am moved by your compassion, and I can only bow in gratitude. I am awestruck once again.

No More Shadows

God is light; in him there is no darkness at all.

1 John 1:5

Oh, the shadows I bring with me are plentiful. They include losses, sins, and worries that stay with me, Lord. I've become comfortable in the dark, but this way of living is taking its toll. Anger and impatience quickly rise when I interact with others. This is not who I am when I embrace my identity as a child of God and dwell in your light. Pride can do such spiritual damage.

Today, with great longing, I make my way to you. First, your light is my beacon to guide me back to your heart and the warmth of your compassion. Then your light is my salvation as shadows disappear and I stand open, vulnerable, and ready to be filled.

Dear Shepherd

*When he saw the crowds, he had compassion
on them, because they were harassed and
helpless, like sheep without a shepherd.*

MATTHEW 9:36

Lord, you see me for the orphaned sheep that I am, and your heart adopts me. You know I can be challenging to keep in the safe confines of your watch, but you love me anyway. Your attention to my helplessness shows me I'm worth the bother and the belief. When I try to find my own way, you call my name tenderly. Your voice stills my spirit like nothing else. All I want is to be closer to the One who can speak my name with such compassion.

Lord, some worldly masters in my life didn't care about my purpose or survival. But with a just and righteous hand, you brought me into your fold and tended to my wounds. Dear Shepherd, I will follow you anywhere.

ANXIETY

May I choose your peace over my
anxiety today, Comforter.

Left with Everything

*Peace I leave with you; my peace I give you. I
do not give to you as the world gives. Do not let
your hearts be troubled and do not be afraid.*

JOHN 14:27

Examine my heart, God. Do you feel the weight of it? I collect worries rather than confront, process, and release them. This isn't a hobby for a healthy life, but how do I stop? And what would fill the space now occupied by this collection? Lord, have I become so used to this ever-present sensation of pressure that I'm hesitant to make a change?

What would have a chance to grow if I gave my difficulties and fears to you instead of accumulating them? The thought of this exchange brightens my mood. Through you and your grace, I can have a heart emptied of stale sorrows. I wouldn't be left with nothing; I would be open to everything that flows from your peace.

You Asked for It

Do not be anxious about anything,
but in every situation,
by prayer and petition, with thanksgiving,
present your requests to God.

PHILIPPIANS 4:6

I will never wear out my welcome when I come to your feet again and again with my requests. (I can't get over this, God.) There's no comparison to your patience. You invite me, without condition or restriction, to bring tear-stained requests along with my praises and thanksgivings.

So here I am again. Not with requests this time but with a muddled sense of brokenness I can't unravel on my own. I would be embarrassed by this mess of an offering—except for the fact that in your mercy, you asked for it.

Surprised

*I remain confident of this: I will see the goodness of the
LORD in the land of the living.
Wait for the LORD; be strong and take
heart and wait for the LORD.*

PSALM 27:13-14

Facing a future surprise triggers worries in me. Anything can happen, God. Don't make me guess. Don't make me wait. Things haven't been so great, and the waiting time inflates worst-case scenarios into mental monsters. Lord, you know I get nervous. I need the assurance of your presence.

When I quit looking up anxiously to see where you are, I become still enough to rest in the Holy Spirit. I have confidence I'll experience the land of the living, a place where my mind isn't divided by the what-ifs while I wait for you. I won't be surprised when I feel your presence, because you have promised to be with me. But I will be amazed by how your goodness renders the waiting useful.

Get Up...Stay

When they had gone, an angel of the Lord appeared to Joseph in a dream. "Get up...take the child and his mother and escape to Egypt. Stay there until I tell you, for Herod is going to search for the child to kill him."

MATTHEW 2:13

You protect your beloved children just as you watched over the Christ child. When I'm unsure about how I fit or where I belong, I can have peace because my identity is born of and etched in your heart. I am yours. You whisper to my spirit when it's time to change direction, move along, stay put, or rest patiently in the place of safety you prepare in advance.

You provide the escape I need *when* I need it. I insistently point to dangers outside my window. Worries darken sky and mind. But in your peaceful way, you call for me to get up and then to escape my anxiety by staying here in the shelter of care you've prepared.

AUTHENTICITY

May I journey toward acceptance
and appreciation of the me
you dreamed into being.

Detours in Discernment

My son...preserve sound judgment and discretion;
they will be life for you, an ornament to grace your neck.
Then you will go on your way in safety,
and your foot will not stumble.

PROVERBS 3:21-23

My thoughts at night have turned toward past choices. Have they caused me to stumble and take a detour away from the path you were pointing out? How did I mess up a year ago? Have I made decisions that undermine who I'm created to be? God, free me from worries that threaten to strangle my hope. Let me preserve sound judgment so it's a source of life for me, an adornment around my neck, an ever-present reminder of your protection as I make my way along *the* way you've carved out for me.

When I'm about to latch onto a worry, help me grab hold of you instead. Let my thoughts be transformed into prayers for wisdom and your leading, Lord.

No Substitutions

*Keep your lives free from the love of money
and be content with what you have,
because God has said, "Never will I leave
you; never will I forsake you."*

HEBREWS 13:5

God, you are the source and provider of true love. I've come to you to be refilled, and you never turn me away. Instead you wow me with abundance. When I can't take in the unending supply of your presence, it's because I've tried to fill up with other versions of love: money, adoration, status. They don't make me content, so I keep adding to them. Some days I'm so weary because all I can do is struggle to feed the longing. But there's no substitution for the love that sates the soul. That love comes from you alone. When I empty myself of the world's substitutions and come to you as an open vessel, you fill me. I'm at peace in a way that surprises me, and I'm thankful. Nothing compares to your faithful presence, Lord.

What Is Good

Do not be conformed to this world, but be transformed by the renewal of your mind, that by testing you may discern what is the will of God, what is good and acceptable and perfect.

ROMANS 12:2 ESV

Help, Lord! So many thoughts that seem false have entered my mind lately. They are, at best, exaggerated in their power and influence. They have weight and form shadows not only in my mind but in my heart. I don't know if I'm being influenced by outside factors and future fears or if these are the thoughts of a renewed mind able to discern what is of you. Are they real? Or are they fabricated warnings that emerge from the dark corners?

I'm ready to commit to following your true way, God—your authentic design for this life of mine. Remove from me any ideas, suspicions, and fears that distract me from your perfect will.

The Feast That Satisfies

*Why spend money on what is not bread,
and your labor on what does not satisfy?
Listen, listen to me, and eat what is good,
and you will delight in the richest fare.*

ISAIAH 55:2

Lord, I'm so hungry for what's real. People speak of authentic living, but finding a personal way to it is impossible unless I seek my identity, nourishment, and purpose in you. Your hands create and provide what is true, good, and righteous. The world offers so many distracting pseudo versions of your *real* provisions. Nobody gets well on fake food, yet it's so easy to spend money on Oreos and not the orange in my quest for satisfaction.

Forgive me for the times I do this same sad swap when choosing spiritual food. Guide me toward what is good and nourishing for my soul. Give me a hunger for your real feast. I want to invest my resources and effort in the pursuit of the delightful fare you've prepared.

GRATITUDE

May I untangle my assortment of worries
so my path to gratitude is unhindered.

Blessed and Uplifted

*Blessed is she who has believed that the
Lord would fulfill his promises to her!*

LUKE 1:45

The moment I allow my worries to fade to the background, your invitation to believe is so compelling that all of me responds. My body relaxes with the gift of your concern. My spirit softens and is ready for wisdom and not fear. And my mind clears and makes room for words of guidance and consolation. I'm blessed and uplifted as you fulfill your promises to me.

When my belief meets your faithfulness, gifts are brought forth. I walk with a confident stride. I don't shy away from what is difficult. And each obstacle that clamors in my mind or rises along my path is met with a deep sense of possibility. These obstacles aren't woes to feed and fuel with more worry; they're opportunities to be grateful for your power and love.

Trading Trouble for Thanksgiving

*Always giving thanks to God the Father for everything,
in the name of our Lord Jesus Christ.*

EPHESIANS 5:20

I haven't quite figured out how to phrase my gratitude for a current concern, though I'm trying to practice the art of being thankful for everything. For *all* things. Even this thing that causes me to stare at the ceiling at two in the morning, that drains my energy and leaves me anxious. I can't believe a single fret has such control, Lord. I want to put this worry in its place, and that place is *not* the place of power. That's your spot.

I'm giving this trouble over to the joy of thanksgiving. If it comes to mind, I'll surrender it to you. Thank you, Lord, for everything that leads me back to knowing and trusting that you are the ruler of my life.

All Creation Celebrates

Shout for joy, you heavens; rejoice, you earth;
burst into song, you mountains!
For the LORD comforts his people and will
have compassion on his afflicted ones.

ISAIAH 49:13

From the deepest sea to the highest peak, your love of details is evident. When I stand among tall pine trees or come across an intricate shell on the beach, I know your nature is to amaze and joyfully create. You care about what you've brought into being. I'm not here by accident; my life matters to you. And the days that present more challenges than victories are not dismissed as insignificant.

I want to sink into the compassion you offer me today. It becomes my hammock from which to view all the beauty you present, if only I will look. And should I pause long enough to listen as well, I'll hear your creation rejoice. Let me join in, Lord. Let me add my voice to the song of appreciation for your care.

Forget the Buckets

*I will make them and the places
surrounding my hill a blessing.
I will send down showers in season;
there will be showers of blessing.*

EZEKIEL 34:26

I watched a friend express deep gratitude for your graces and realized how rarely I gather the blessings you shower down. When the winds stir, I take cover. I troubleshoot and make plans to protect myself from what might come. I watch for a troubled sky. These are the choices of an anxious heart, not one eager to receive blessing.

Winds are gaining momentum now, but instead of closing the windows to secure my shelter, I'm going to grab buckets and rush outside my comfort zone to gather the many blessings: family moments, unexpected opportunities, authentic connections, nature's inspiration, and so much more. Forget the buckets. I'll collect your mercies with my open heart and with palms lifted in praise.

POWERLESSNESS

May I reframe my weakness as an
invitation to live in your mighty power.

Wrestling Worries

*"Not by might nor by power, but by my
Spirit," says the LORD Almighty.*

ZECHARIAH 4:6

’m exhausted, Lord. With effort and strain and ridiculous tactics, I try to wrestle my worries into submission. Sometimes I catch myself mid-struggle and laugh at how earnest I am in my efforts to overpower my difficulties. Has this ever worked for me? No. Have you told me that my spiritual and life struggles will be overcome in my power? No. But here I am again, down for the count and growing more frustrated by the minute.

When I finally break down, I surrender. Only by your Spirit will my human fragments be made whole. With great relief, I stop trying to be my own redeemer.

Spotlight on Your Power

*Therefore I will boast all the more gladly
about my weaknesses,
so that Christ's power may rest on me.*

2 Corinthians 12:9

The desire to be loved by people can be such fodder for worry. I analyze and criticize my choices and behaviors. I experience horror as each social fail or public stumble manifests. At night I relive these scenes and chastise myself. I worry that no one will take my power seriously after such evidence of weakness.

Then, in the stillness that follows wearisome worry sessions, you show me the scenes in a new light. I see you lift me up not by elevating my personal power but by carrying me in your own. I see the friend or stranger observing my vulnerable moment without judgment and with buoyed personal hope; they have proof that our acceptance and care are real. I'm so humbled and relieved. My life at its best puts the spotlight on your power, Lord.

Celebrating Weakness

*For Christ's sake, I delight in weaknesses, in insults,
in hardships, in persecutions, in difficulties.
For when I am weak, then I am strong.*

2 CORINTHIANS 12:10

Start the party, Lord. Unleash the delight. My weaknesses and I are here, front and center. Everyone in my world is invited. From the neighbors I barely know to the friends who faithfully walk beside me in both times of trouble and times of blessing. I can handle onlookers who see firsthand my breakdowns and character flaws and spirals of anxiety because my every weakness is a witness to your mercy.

I don't want to shy away from celebrating the raw places of my existence, because your perfection and grace are illuminated there. People might come to get a glimpse of my small disasters, but they stay for your salvation show. I'm good with that.

A Show of Might

Summon your power, God;
show us your strength, our God,
as you have done before.

PSALM 68:28

'm falling into your strength with full abandon. I feel like the kid at the playground telling all the others how powerful my dad is—"Just wait until you see him!" I want to show my family and friends your might and mercy, God. They've witnessed my powerlessness and my need for healing and hope. They've seen me tumble completely into your care. What other choice could I ever make? I want to be in my Father's arms. This is where wounds are mended and scars are acknowledged and soothed in love.

Show all of us your strength, Lord. I'll show everyone just who my amazing Father is, praying that they'll want to run into your arms too.

MEANING

May I allow worries to fall away as you
shape a life of spiritual significance.

A Place to Talk

The hand of the LORD was on me there,
and he said to me,
"Get up and go out to the plain, and
there I will speak to you."

EZEKIEL 3:22

Lord, I feel the tug at my heart and nearly perceive a physical tug at my arm as you pull, pull, pull me toward you for conversation. My mind has been preoccupied with questions about purpose and what I should be doing with my life. Such concerns can take over all things, including my prayer life. You don't chide me or turn from me during my intense rounds of reflection. Instead you touch me and coax me to come away with you to a place we can talk about all these things.

We have so much to share, so I will meet you— whether in my bedroom before the day's demands holler, in my car during the lunch hour, or along a quiet stretch of trail at dusk. I can't wait, Lord.

What Endures

People, despite their wealth, do not endure.

PSALM 49:12

God, set my heart in rhythm with eternity. I follow you through my days with gratitude for each day that comes and goes. On earth, what begins will eventually end. The money I earn and set aside won't last. The plans I make during rich conversations with friends will unfold in this way or that, yet they won't carry me beyond my lifetime. You will.

It's freeing to lightly hold the strands that tether me to the physical world. It's a relief to not value the meaningless things. What does endure is what matters most and what holds true, that my soul, my deepest being, will be with you one day. And when that time arrives, today's concern about whether I have enough will fade to nothing because I will be in your presence. *That's* everything.

Use This Life

*Offer yourselves to God as those who have
been brought from death to life;
and offer every part of yourself to him as
an instrument of righteousness.*

ROMANS 6:13

I choose to be an offering to you, Lord. As this heart beats, the life it fuels is yours to use in the world—even in my small world. Guide me to conversations with those who need a spirited word. Change the course of my direction so I reach destinations plotted in your wisdom. Use my times of contemplation to restore my energy and prepare me for interactions and actions.

God, whatever is useful in me for your purpose today, it's yours. (You knew this, but you wait for me to catch up.) What part of me is untapped or shut down? Where am I divided and confused? Deliver these areas from death to life so they're open for your will to flow through them.

I Can't Explain It

Dear friends, do not be surprised
at the fiery ordeal that has come on you to test you,
as though something strange were happening to you.

1 PETER 4:12

Am I on a bad reality show? Or maybe on an episode of *The Twilight Zone*? God, so much that's hard to accept, to believe, has happened lately. I mentally journey back through the past months to figure out why life took such a strange turn. I had a plan I thought was from you, but recent complications are blocking my view to possibility. I wish this were a TV show, so I could fast-forward to a resolution that might redeem the nights of worry.

But, Lord, *you* redeem this trial through your wisdom and knowing, and you give it meaning. Even when you don't reveal all the answers, your grace anchors me in the hope I need for this moment and for the next. There is significance in even this strange turn of events. I can't explain it, but I certainly believe it.

RESTORATION

May my pursuit of wholeness be
along the narrow path of faith.

Seedlings

*Truly I tell you, if you have faith as small as a
mustard seed, you can say to this mountain,
"Move from here to there," and it will move.
Nothing will be impossible for you.*

MATTHEW 17:20

It's moving day. I'm ready and eager, and I'm trusting your promises. A seemingly impossible situation is rising and expanding. It's become a mountain up ahead. I've given enough worry over to how I might go around it or over it, so now I want this foreboding obstruction relocated away from my path and my view. Way over there would be nice.

Let me turn to the seedlings of possibility in me. These are enough, because your power is mighty and restores even broken faith. I believe you when you say the measure of my faith needn't match the size of the obstacle to make miracles happen in your name. You let me do the honors: "Move from here to there," I cry, and I watch expectantly for the impossible to become possible.

Even That?

God has taken away my disgrace.
GENESIS 30:23

I am a hoarder of worries and past mistakes. This life rubble fills the rooms of my mind and heart. I side-step the piles and try to be productive at work, engage in conversation with a friend, or seek your direction, God. Sometimes I throw past transgressions into a mental box marked "deal with later." But, Lord, I know I can't deal with them on my own. I need your help to remove clutter from my spirit.

You ask me to give each transgression to you as I am able. You speak of how useful an open, forgiven heart is. Patiently, you wait. As I point to a past regret and ask, "Even this one?" you assure me that, yes, even that one can be surrendered to your grace so that my path is restored.

Pared Down to Purpose

*He cuts off every branch in me that bears no fruit,
while every branch that does bear fruit he
prunes so that it will be even more fruitful.*

JOHN 15:2

God, you know I'm not always eager to have you prepare me for growth. I stubbornly hold on to weaknesses. I do the same with strengths you reveal as needing to be released because they aren't useful for my calling. It's difficult to let go of something that's working or reaping abundance, but the growth you lead me toward requires me to say no to whatever isn't bearing the fruit you call into *my* life.

The process of simplifying can be painful, but through it you restore my purpose. I will harvest your hope for my circumstances. Already I can taste the sweetness of all that will be produced in my life when I offer it to the master Gardener.

Restored Strength

*The God of all grace, who called you to his
eternal glory in Christ, after you have suffered
a little while, will himself restore you and
make you strong, firm and steadfast.*

1 Peter 5:10

During this time of stress, I must exercise my trust in you, God. My weariness does not equal weakness, but to believe this, I must listen closely to you or I might lose the hope to persevere. These current difficulties generate worries that tax my energy and lead me to question everything I'm doing. Yet I witness how they're also conditioning my faith and ushering me toward restoration and spiritual growth.

Even if I question whether what I'm doing and how I'm responding are right, I receive great comfort knowing I need not question whether what *you* are doing is right. Your grace will restore me. This journey is not about getting back to "normal" but about getting back to you.

COURAGE

May I surrender my timidity in
the presence of your strength.

I Accept This Delivery

I have begun to deliver...begin to conquer and possess.
DEUTERONOMY 2:31

I look confident to others, but the resumé I keep up-to-date isn't about achievements and promotions; it's filled with the risk not taken, the leap of faith squelched, and the job not pursued. You know these items, God, because they also make up my list of laments in darker times.

When I trust you, I can let go of this resumé of disappointments. You've already overcome anything I'm afraid of, so what's left for me to dwell on with fear after you deliver that power to my life? I receive your mighty grace, Lord. In that grace and with you, those regrets are conquered. I accept this COD—courage over disappointment—with faith and hope.

Only Grace

*Then Jesus told his disciples a parable to show them
that they should always pray and not give up.*

LUKE 18:1

I'm overcome with gratitude for how you tend to me as your child, God. You encourage me with comfort when stresses bring me to my knees. I feel your presence all around me. Your words to my heart never dismiss my heartbreaks or woes. Instead you tell me to press on in faith and to always pray with hope.

You direct me toward awe and tell me to keep going. Not once have I felt I was alone in this. Abba, you share stories to remind me of the times you carried and guided me. Only grace is in your words, never disappointment. The abundant mercy you give allows me to never give up.

Courage to Pray

*LORD, let the promise you have made concerning
your servant and his house be established forever.
Do as you promised... You, my God, have revealed
to your servant that you will build a house for him.
So your servant has found courage to pray to you.*

1 CHRONICLES 17:23,25

I hold on to worries in different ways. Some I grip with such force that I wonder if my heart will ever release them. Others I feed and fuel with hypotheticals, hoping to figure out the puzzle of my future. Lord, I became certain that I needed to be the one in control. At some point in time, I started to believe this handling of worries was a way to be strong. Even courageous. But I was acting without faith.

I want to live with a loose grip on my worries and a tight hold on belief in the purpose you build for me. Real courage is born when I pray to you, God. When I lay bare my raw needs and open my heart to your faithfulness.

Not What I Requested

See, I have refined you, though not as silver;
I have tested you
in the furnace of affliction.

ISAIAH 48:10

I don't always want to accept how things work. By "things" I mean your ways, God. I'm grateful you don't try to cheer me up with false hope. Instead you promise to be beside me. You vow that a new version of me will emerge after I've been tested in the flames fueled by unease and doubts.

This is not the journey I prayed for. This is not a story line I dreamed of playing out. But I've witnessed your miracles and beautiful connections in the middle of the hardest tests. As I wipe the sweat from my brow, I realize I'm different from how I was in the beginning. I've accepted how these things work. By "things," I mean your indestructible, refining love and power.

TRUST

May I unwind my worried mind
and trust your clear way of peace.

Not Just Anyone

*He who forms the mountains, who creates the wind,
and who reveals his thoughts to mankind, who turns
dawn to darkness, and treads on the heights of the
earth—the LORD God Almighty is his name.*

AMOS 4:13

You are the one who hears and holds my prayers,
God. On many days I've mumbled my laments
and told myself that nobody was listening, that nobody
cared. I forgot who you were—the One who forms
mountains and reveals his thoughts to his creations.
You also *listen* to the thoughts of your creations. You
know the small, large, and exaggerated worries that
darken my mind.

Today, if I'm tempted to fret rather than be free,
I'll remember to whom I'm talking and entrusting my
circumstances. And when I'm about to turn a molehill
into a mountain, I'll laugh at myself and remind my
spirit that only *you* make mountains. That's not my
job, even when I pretend it is.

No More Safe Mode

*May the God of hope fill you with all joy and peace
as you trust in him, so that you
may overflow with hope by the power of the Holy Spirit.*

ROMANS 15:13

Empty me, God. Then please, oh please, fill me with your joy. In the busyness of my day, my head is filled with worries, and my heart carries the broken pieces of old plans. I want to know what it's like to be filled with your joy and to trust you for my every hope, my every need.

I'm grateful that you want to pour new life into me and sate me with purpose.

I've been living this old life so long that I know it backward and forward, yet I no longer want to remain in safe mode. I want to empty myself of old plans and create space for the peace and power of the Holy Spirit.

Trusting Your Will for Me

Be still before the LORD and wait patiently for him; do not fret when people succeed in their ways, when they carry out their wicked schemes.

PSALM 37:7

Lord, you know the inner workings of my heart and mind. Some things I would like to hide from you, but at the end of the day, I'm grateful that I can come before you and lay my burdens, secrets, sins, and faulty thoughts at your feet.

Today I come clean with my envy of someone who has tasted acclaim. But the acclaim came at the expense of others, and that's not how I want to succeed. Forgive me for being distracted by this example and for my envy as I await the pieces of my own life to fit together and make sense. I trust you, Lord. I experience no gain when I worry about the rise of others. I gain only when I focus on living out your good and perfect will for me.

Wait for It

*The revelation awaits an appointment time... Though it
linger, wait for it; it will certainly
come and will not delay.*

HABAKKUK 2:3

I have peace for the first time in a long time. I'm still
waiting for your direction, but my anxiousness has
been soothed. I'm taking full breaths, and my body is at
ease. My circumstances haven't changed, but my perspective has. I know your vision will unfold; I no longer
wait for my situation to become perfect or my needs to
disappear; I wait for your promises and your timing. I
might still fumble through this season as I tend to the
needs of family, finances, or next steps, yet I wait for
you and on you with trust.

I know you aren't stalling or ignoring me. You're
inviting me to walk with the companions of faith and
hope as you unfold your promises in your time.

About the Author

Hope Lyda is an author whose devotionals, novels, and prayer books, including the popular *One-Minute Prayers® for Women* and *Life as a Prayer*, have sold over one million copies. Her inspirational books reflect her desire to embrace and deepen faith while journeying to God's mystery and wonder.

Hope has worked in publishing for more than 20 years, writing and coming alongside other writers to help them shape their heart messages and mine their experiences to connect with others. As a trained spiritual director, she loves to help others enter God's presence and pay attention to their authentic, unique life and purpose. Her greatest joy is to find ways to extend these invitations through the written word and writing exercises.

Contact Hope at hopelyda@gmail.com

Learn more at www.hopelyda.com

Follow on Instagram @hopelydawrites

MORE FAVORITE READS FROM HOPE LYDA

AVAILABLE ONLY AS E-BOOK